ONE THING YOU LACK

Stephen Lavoe

ONE THING YOU LACK

by

<u>Stephen Lavoe</u>

Unless otherwise indicated, all Scripture quotations are taken
from the New King James Version of the Bible.
Contents of this book or cover may not be reprinted for
commercial gain or profit.

Printed in 2005 by Stephen Lavoe

<u>U.S.A. Address</u>
Action Christian Center Int'l
4395 Byron Avenue, Bronx, NY 10466
Telephone (718) 324-5845

<u>Africa Address</u>
Action Christian Center Int'l
P.O. Box 373, U.S.T.
Kumasi, Ghana, West Africa

I.S.B.N. 1890430-19-6

Printed by

Triumph Publishing
PO Box 690158
Bronx, NY 10469

CONTENTS

Dedication

Foreword

Introduction

CHAPTERS

DEDICATION

This book is dedicated to all young ministers who are devoted, anointed and zealous to do God's work. It is written for them to know that there are some things they lack and should always submit to their Senior Pastors or Spiritual Father. It is also dedicated to my beloved daughter Evelyn A. Lavoe.

It is written so that the "one thing you lack" should be identified and worked on in the journey of life, as you follow the footsteps of Christ Jesus your Savior.

FOREWORD

Throughout history and in recent years, we have heard and witnessed men and women of great valor and power, including ministers of the Gospel of Christ, whose lives were either cut short or were not able to fulfill their mission here on earth, because of one thing they lacked. One of such men was Alexander the Great. Alexander the Great was one of the greatest Generals of all time. He studied under great men including Aristotle. The Prophet Daniel, in his prophetic writings, spoke about the lightning speed with which Alexander the Great would conquer the ancient world (Daniel 7:6; 8:5). Surely, in swiftness he broke the Persian power and became a powerful leader and master of the Ancient world. However, at a very tender age of 33, Alexander's life was cut short. His death is still shrouded in mystery to this very day. Many historians, however, believe that his ego, ruthlessness, and drinking problem made him vulnerable to his enemies.

As a minister and counselor, I have sat down with many people who had good and bright aspirations and yet found themselves sitting before me disappointed, dejected, and sometimes depressed for unfulfilled dreams and aspirations gone awry. They would say, "Oh, if I had only done this one thing right." That confession is always true. There is always one small thing that stands between us and the fulfillment of our dreams. Realizing our short comings, accepting them, and working on them would catapult us to the fulfillment of our desired dreams. However, failure to do so would cause pain, disappointment, and unfulfilled dreams.

I highly applaud my colleague and friend, Rev. Dr. Stephen Lavoe for obeying God and writing this much needed book, "One Thing You Lack." He has rightly indicated in the book, that there is "one thing lacking" in everyone of us, for there is no perfect man who ever lived on this planet, with the exception of Jesus Christ our Lord. I truly concur with Dr. Lavoe, for we all have our strengths and weaknesses. We all need to upgrade our lives by eliminating the "One Thing" that might cut our vision short or hinder our progress, and finding the "One Thing" that would propel us to finish our course and finish it well. The great Apostle Paul found his "One Thing," and worked on it, and as a result, he was able to fulfill his goals for the Lord. Paul declared,

> "Not that I have already attained, or am already perfected; but I press on, that I may lay hold of that for which Christ Jesus has also laid hold of me. Brethren, I do not count myself to have apprehended; but one thing I do, forgetting those things which are behind and reaching forward to those things which are ahead, I press toward the goal for the prize of the upward call of God in Christ Jesus" (Philippians 3:12-14).

I highly recommend this book to everyone, especially believers. It is my prayer that as you read, God would speak to you and help you to locate your "One Thing You Lack" to help fulfill your dreams.

Rev. Dr. Isaac M. Arku
Founder & President
The Light of the World Christian Ministries International
East Fishkill, New York

INTRODUCTION

Precious Friend,

I was awakened in the middle of the night on January 15, 2004 at 3:09 am. While I was seeking the face of God I had this prompting in my spirit, "One Thing You Lack" may be stopping the heavens from opening in your life. I begun to search the Word of God regarding the "one thing" I lacked, whether positive or negative in my own life.

I also discovered the "one thing" some great men and women of God throughout scripture lacked in their lives and how it either distracted, delayed, or destroyed their destinies, regarding the purpose of God for their lives.

You may be gifted with the Word of Knowledge; you may be anointed with fresh oil, so much that tangible and visible miracles follow you each day, yet, there is still "One Thing You Lack."

The paradox of the "One Thing You Lack" is that, what you lack could be something positive that you have to work hard on in order to incorporate that element or virtue into your life, or what you lack could be something negative which has already become part and parcel of your life. It is a pattern of behavior, which has become your attitude and is slowly, but surely, eating the best out of you. And all you are saying is, "As for me, this is how

I am." No! You can change. I am optimistic that you can eliminate that negative lifestyle and replace it with the positive aspect of whatever you might be lacking.

Notice what God Almighty is saying here:

> "My people are destroyed for lack of knowledge. Because you have rejected knowledge, I also will reject you from being priest for Me; because you have forgotten the law of your God, I also will forget your children" (Hosea 4:6).

What these people lacked here was knowledge of the Law of God.

The "One Thing You Lack," whether positive or negative, can delay you, deny you of opened doors, or destroy you.

As you journey through this awesome book, may the Spirit of Christ give you illumination to comprehend each page, to grant you insight and foresight to enable you to take another step forward in fulfilling your assignment on planet earth.

As you study this book, do so with an open mind. May you locate the "One Thing You Lack," removing all limitations, correcting things and committing to change all that is necessary to become a blessing to those who come your way.

Dr. Stephen Lavoe

Chapter One

The People Is One

A story was told of three young, energetic, strong men. One day these three brothers were informed that a friend of theirs who was not sick, had died tragically. These three men were so mad about the sudden death of their friend that they decided to search for Mr. Death and kill him.

On their way, they met an old man and they asked him, "Sir, a lot of young people are dying. How come you are so old and still alive?" The old man replied, "I told Mr. Death to kill me, I even begged him to, but he wouldn't do it. That is why I am still around."

The young men asked, "Do you know where to find Mr. Death?" The old man replied, "Oh, yes! Mr. Death is in the forest under that big tree."

The three men went on their search into the particular forest and when they found the big tree, they started digging under the tree in search of Mr. Death. They dug and dug, and after many hours, they found a big pot of gold bars. To their surprise, their search had turned into a fortune.

Because of the journey and the digging, they ran out of water and they could hardly stand on their feet. One of the men suggested that the youngest should go to the city and buy them water and food while the other two would watch the gold bars.

The younger one went to the city, and after getting the water and food he started thinking how wonderful it could be if he got all the money to himself. An evil

idea came to him and he bought poison to kill the other two brothers. When he got closer to where they were, he poisoned the water. One thing he did not know was that his brothers were plotting against him.

After the younger one went to buy the water and food, the two who were left behind started thinking how incredible it would be if they could keep the gold bars to themselves. So, they plotted that when the younger one came they would kill him and the money would be theirs alone.

Immediately as the youngest brother returned and was putting down the water and food, the two older brothers jumped on him and beat him to death. They then sat down to drink and eat, not knowing that their younger brother had poisoned the water in his quest to have the gold bars to himself. After eating and drinking, both of them also died.

> *You may love each other – but when money comes between you, it will prove whether your love is genuine or fake.*

These three men were knitted together as family; they were there for each other, protected each other and had one goal together. They said they loved each other but **one thing destroyed them all – GREED.**

And the "one thing they lacked" was "Agape Love," an unconditional love for each other, whether they had money or not.

In your journey of life, locate the "one thing" that could destroy your relationship with friends, family or loved ones.

> *GREED – was the one thing they did not avoid.*
>
> *AGAPE LOVE – was the "one thing they lacked"*

They wanted to get Mr. Death and kill him. Unfortunately, death struck them, unnoticed, from the opposite direction. Fortune turned them into fools, and finally they ended as failures.

> *A fortune of God brought them Failure.*

Nimrod's Story

> "And the whole earth was of **one language,** and of **one speech.** And it came to pass, as they journeyed from the east, that they found a plain in the land of Shiner; and they dwelt there. And they said one to another, Go to, let us make brick and burn them thoroughly. And they had brick for stone, and slime had they for mortar" (Genesis 11:1-3).

> "And the Lord said, Behold, **the people is one**, and they have one language; and this they begin to do: and now nothing will be restrained from them, which they have imagined to do" (Genesis 11:6).

"The people is one" may sound like a wrong grammatical statement, but God used it to prove a point and I love it. They were bound together and fastened together, so much so, that nothing could pull them apart.

- The people is one.
- They have one language.
- They have one vision – to build a tower.
- They have one goal – to make a name for themselves.

That was until one word they didn't know struck them – *"Confusion"* or *"Babel."*

Ironically, the city they built was called "Babel." Historians have said that the city was built nicely. Amazingly, they might have finished building the city first and then came to the tower - the first sky scraper in the world.

They built the tower towards heaven in a united spirit. This proves the incredible power of unity in a group of people.

The leader of that great city was called "Nimrod the Mighty," a strong militant black man. Oh, yes, he was a black man; let me prove it to you.

> "The sons of Ham were Cush, Mizraim, Put, and Canaan. The sons of Cush were Seba, Havilah, Sabtah, Raamah, and Sabtechah; and the sons of Raamah were Sheba and Dedan. Cush begot Nimrod; he began to be a mighty one on the earth. He was a mighty hunter before the Lord; therefore it is said, "Like Nimrod the mighty hunter before the Lord." And the beginning of his kingdom was Babel, Erech, Accad, and Calneh, in the land of Shinar" (Genesis 10:6-10).

The word "Cush" or "Cushite" means:

a)   Burnt face or black
b)   Dark skin

Ham was the one most people said Noah cursed but that is not "TRUE," not at all. Although Ham was the one who saw his father's nakedness, Noah did not curse him; rather, he cursed his last born son called "Canaan."

The point is that Ham's first born was called Cush. Cush was a black man and his first born son's name was Nimrod. Therefore, "Nimrod the Mighty One" was a black man.

This does not mean that black people are better than other races. Absolutely not! This is just to let those who don't know understand that this leader was a black man. Nimrod did not only build a city, he built cities, and established a kingdom and a civilization.

"Nimrod the Mighty One" was an architect and an engineer. He built the first sky scraper and established a kingdom, and he was the King of that kingdom Gen 10:10).

Nimrod, the black man, made some mistakes; however, there was something great in him.

There Are Great Things In Black People Too

The problem with "Nimrod the Mighty One" and his associates was that they tried to make a name for themselves. And what was that name?

 a) We will not scatter on the earth as God wanted.
 b) We have built a tower into heaven right under God's nose.

"We have defied God's word and are successful." This was the name they wanted to make for themselves.

I want you to notice some important things here.

- There was nothing wrong with the cities they built.
- There was nothing wrong with the towers they built.

Rather, there was something wrong with their "ego" when they decided to defy the authority of God and make a name for themselves - Pride. "Pride goes before destruction" (Proverbs. 16:18).

> "And the Lord said, "Indeed the people are one and they all have one language, and this is what they begin to do; now nothing that they propose to do will be withheld from them" (Genesis 11:6).

- When a family is one,
- When a community is one,
- When a church is one,
- When a company is one,
- **There is no power on earth that can stop them from achieving what they have imagined to do – VISION.**

Vision

Vision is different from a goal. A goal is what you want to **achieve**. Vision is what you want to **establish**.

They rallied around Nimrod's vision and they built cities and established a kingdom. The result was success, until "one thing they lacked" hit them like a hit man.

The "one thing they lacked" was God's divine approval. And because they lacked that, confusion struck them from out of nowhere.

> *Confusion is the half-sister to Chaos.*

Anytime confusion raises its ugly head you must know that chaos is inevitable. These people had everything going for them until what they could not combat hit them, and chaos was the end result.

I know of a strong, well-organized church with more than two thousand members in their congregation in New York City. This is a church you could say "The People is One." That was until one tiny insignificant element of confusion hit them and they were not able to combat that virus. Emotions erupted and intelligence was buried, and within three weeks that mighty church came crumbling down. In fact, the whole church collapsed, and the doors of the building were locked.

The "one thing" the church lacked was "genuine patience," because patience is the glue that allows love to bind people together.

> ***Don't Let Your Emotions Override***
> ***Your Intelligence.***

As you continue reading you will realize that no matter how well:

- You may be organized in your family
- You may be organized in your church
- You may be organized in your company

There is "one thing you lack," and I trust that the spirit of God will give you illumination of that one thing in order for you to avoid chaos and disaster when it comes knocking at your door.

Apply this to your own life.

Life Application

Identify GREED and SELFISHNESS in your own personal life. Pray and work effectively to get rid of it, and replace them with the "one thing you lack" – Agape Love and God's approval, or else you are not going anywhere in life.

Chapter Two

One Thing You Know

An atheist in a small town stood up to interrupt a preacher in a town hall, saying, "There is no God," and the whole service ended up in chaos.   On another occasion a young preacher went to that same small town to preach.   While he was in the middle of his message, the same atheist showed up and went straight to the platform, interrupting the preacher, saying "Young man, there is no God!"   A dialogue between them transpired like this...

Young Preacher: One thing I know is that God is real.
Atheist: One thing I also know is that there is no God.
Young Preacher: Let me prove what I know to you.

The young preacher took an orange and showed it to the whole crowd gathered there and he sliced the orange into four and asked the atheist to take one slice of the orange and eat it.

Atheist: No way, I won't eat the orange.
Young Preacher: Okay, I will eat the orange myself.

	(After eating, he asked him) How does the orange taste, is it sweet or bitter?
Atheist:	Why do you ask me? I didn't taste the orange. How should I know if it is sweet or bitter?
Young Preacher:	Thank you for saying that you don't know, and you are right.
Atheist:	What is your point? This orange has nothing to do with our conversation about the existence of God.
Young Preacher:	Oh, yes it does. God is just like the orange. Unless you taste him you will never know whether He is real or not. If I tell you that the orange is sweet or bitter you will not be convinced until you taste the orange for yourself.

"I have tested God, just like the orange and I know he is real. The Bible says, "Oh, taste and see that the Lord is good" (Psalm 34:8).

This analogy hit the atheist to the core of his being.

Atheist:	Goodness, this is a powerful analogy. Young Preacher, please help me. I want to taste God so that **I will know the reality** of his existence!

The atheist tasted that day, and the "one thing he lacked" was that "God is real."

The Strategy of Knowing

- What do you know?
- How do you know it?
- What is the proof of your knowing?

- *Knowing is experiential*

- *Knowing is an encounter*

- *Knowing is when reality sets in*

- *Knowing is when you are convinced about something beyond a reasonable doubt.*

Dr. Oral Roberts said, and I quote: "Most of the time you may not be able to explain what you know to your critics, but you just know that you know, <u>and your know knows it is real</u>."

For example, in the case that you experienced an electrical shock, you know how it feels, but you can't explain, in depth, to your critics how you feel. They will have to experience it for themselves.

> *Knowing is Experiential but sometimes*
>
> *you can't explain it to your critics.*

This young preacher knew that God was real and he used an orange to prove it, and an atheist was convinced. In response he knelt down and asked for help so that he could taste and prove that God was real for himself.

The Blind Man's Incident

> "He answered and said, "Whether He is a sinner or not I do not know. One thing I know: that though I was blind, now I see" (John 9:25).

The above scripture has to do with the miraculous healing of a blind man. Call it an interrogation or hot exchange of words between this blind man, his neighbors and the Pharisees. Some of these people believed he was actually blind because they knew him. Others didn't believe he was truly blind so they brought him to his parents.

> *One Thing I Know,*
>
> *I was Blind,*
>
> *but now I see!*

The Jews did not believe the fact that this man was blind before and had received his sight until they called his parents and questioned them.

> "But the Jews did not believe concerning him, that he had been blind and received his sight, until they

called the parents of him who had received his sight. And they asked them, saying, "Is this your son, who you say was born blind? How then does he now see?" His parents answered them and said, "We know that this is our son, and that he was born blind" (John 9:18-20).

Types of Knowing

There are three different types of knowing:

a) Knowing by experience – Physical
b) Intellectual knowledge – Mental exposure through Education
c) Spiritual knowledge – By Revelation or Illumination

The parents of the blind man said, "*We know* this is our son (physical), but whatever made him see, *we don't know.*"

Listen, there are things you may know in this life, and at the same time, regardless of your education, there are other things that you will not know.

Physical Knowledge
- Knowing by physical experience
- Knowing by the use of one of your five senses (e.g. sight)
- Knowing by being at a place

For example, visiting the tomb of Jesus in Jerusalem or the site of the World Trade Center, physically, you know it as vivid and real.

Intellectual Knowledge

Intellectual knowledge is good and great. You may go to school, a university, take other courses, add value to your skill or get a degree with flying colors. I encourage you to aspire for intellectual knowledge and excel (read at least two books a month).

But, no matter what your qualification or intellectual background, you will not know everything by logic or intellectual achievements.

Spiritual Knowledge

Spiritual knowledge is an encounter that takes place in your spirit being. It is a revolution that overshadows your spirit being and brings you to a place of illumination. Spiritual knowledge brings a remarkable experience of change into your life. Spiritual knowledge is experienced through the process called being "Born Again" (John 3:1-7).

Deception of Spiritual Knowledge

To be deceived regarding spiritual things is very easy to happen. But, patience is the key that allows deception to reveal itself.

Your spiritual knowledge or experience must have:
  a)   A sure foundation   (Matthew 7:24-27)
  b)   Physical proof   (Matthew 7:16-20)

c)   Facts from fiction (1 Corinthians 15:3-7)

> *Patience allows deception to reveal itself.*

Many people want to excel spiritually but have unfortunately fallen shipwrecked through deception. Spirituality does not mean that you should be weird or spooky.

You don't have to light **seven red or black candles**, sprinkle special water or oil, or use an **incantation** book to be spiritual. These are **deceptions.**

- Spirituality is not ritualistic.
- Spirituality has no secrets.
- Spirituality should not always be a mystery.
- Spirituality should not always have dos and don'ts.
- Spirituality should not be something you are afraid of.

If your spirituality has some of these conditions, then you have fallen into deception. You can be spiritual and yet be simple.

> *You can be Spiritual and yet – Simple*

One thing you must know is that being spiritual is not something that you should be scared of. Jesus was the most spiritual man ever and yet he lived a simple down-to-earth-life, here on earth, so that we can follow his footsteps.

> "Then Jesus said to those Jews who believed Him, 'If you abide in My word, you are My disciples indeed. And you shall know the truth, and the truth shall make you free'" (John 8:31-32).

A literal truth does not make one free. Until you know the truth you will not benefit from the freedom it possesses.

After reading the above scripture in my church one day, I asked the congregation, "How many of you think **the truth will make you free?**" To my surprise, every hand went straight up. I asked them to put down their hands and listen to me carefully before putting up their hands again. I slowly asked the question again, "How many of you think the truth shall make you free?" Most of the hands went up again. I told them, "All of you were wrong, because the truth does not make you free." The auditorium went quiet.

I continued to explain to them that, in 1860 President Abraham Lincoln signed a Bill called the Emancipation Proclamation, which meant that every slave in the US working in the fields, homes and on plantations were FREE.

- The Bill was the truth
- The Bill was hanging in the White House

But, after three or four years, many slaves were still working on plantations in Delaware, West Virginia and other states. The Bill was the truth, they were free to walk out on their white masters anytime, but they didn't know the truth.

Therefore, a literal truth cannot make you free; rather, it is the truth you know that makes you free.

> ***Truth does not make you free!***
>
> ***It is the truth you know that makes you free!***

This is how the scripture verse should actually read. "You shall know the truth, and <u>the truth you know shall</u> make you free!"

- ***Knowing eliminates ignorance.***

- ***Knowing removes limitations on you.***

- ***Knowing awakens your understanding capacity. You can then operate in boldness and confidence because your capacity to understand is awakened.***

The Jewish people were still in bondage under the Mosaic laws and their traditions, so they were not free.

- They knew the Mosaic Laws
- They knew the tradition of the Elders
- They knew the Jewish traditions

But "one thing they lacked" – they didn't know the Messiah of Israel.

Do you deeply know and understand?
- Salvation
- Justification
- Holy Spirit Baptism (and speaking in tongues)
- Tithing and Giving
- Forgiveness
- Intercession
- Commitment to the local church
- Honoring and respecting your Spiritual Father (your Pastor)

Please get to know and understand the above topics just like you know your own name. When you do, your destiny will then be transformed. Friend, please understand that Christianity, or your walk with God, is not a hundred meter race, rather it is a marathon!

Don't rush, don't run. Take your time, and slowly but surely learn these things. Stay under authority for your time of elevation shall come.

> *Christianity is not a hundred meter race,*
>
> *rather it is a Marathon!*

This is why Paul the Apostle, the veteran, still wanting to know Christ more than anything else, vocalized these profound words:

> "That I may know Him and the power of His resurrection, and the fellowship of His sufferings, being conformed to His death" (Philippians 3:10).

Paul was not saying that he did not know Christ and therefore wanted to know him – No! That is not what he meant.

Dr. Myles Monroe of Bahamas Faith Ministry, a great man of God once said, "The more I study the Bible deeply, the more I realize I don't know it."

It is paramount to understand that, before Paul made that powerful statement he had previously penned these words.

a)   Things that were gain to me
b)   I count all things lost
c)   And be found in him

Paul had given up a lot of things – his fame, power and prestige for the sake of Christ. This was authentic proof that he knew him. And yet, he said, "That I may know him."

Question – What kind of knowing was he talking about here?

Paul's Spiritual Resume

1) Paul met Jesus on the road to Damascus.
2) He was called an Apostle to the gentile nations.
3) He had established many churches in Asia Minor.
4) He ordained many ministers and pastors into the ministry.
5) Many miracles followed his ministry.
6) He proclaimed Christ before kings, governors and leaders.
7) He raised the dead, commanded cripples to walk and much more.

Amazingly, he looked beyond all of his achievements and said, "That I may know him and the power of his resurrection..." I believe he was talking about a deeper relationship in knowing Christ!

Deep Calls for Deep

> "Deep calls unto deep at the noise of Your waterfalls; All Your waves and billows have gone over me" (Psalm 42:7).

When you fish on the surface of shallow waters you won't get anything. But, when you move into the deep water you will experience a great catch. To encounter great things from the Lord you have got to dig deep into your inner man before you can get deep into the Lord.

When Paul said, "That I may know him," he was saying, "I want to get deep into myself to discover the deep things," (to know the power of his resurrection).

I believe the Apostle Paul was saying, "I know that man called Christ but I don't know him enough or as deep as I should know him."

Paul's resume and great accomplishments in the Kingdom of God were indescribable, yet there was "one thing" he thought he lacked - a deeper and greater anointing in his walk with God.

In your quest for knowing him, understand that spiritual knowing is not instantaneous, it is a daily progressive effort. Jesus said, "If you continue in my word, then are you my disciples indeed." A continual attitude is the authentic proof of knowing him.

> *A Continual Attitude is the*
> *Concrete Effort of Knowing.*

Life Application

Let this be your heart's cry. Tell the Lord this is the "one thing that I lack," but from today I want to know you more and more, and the power of your resurrection.

Chapter Three

One Thing I Desire

A company manager was having a discussion with one of his supervisors and the manager said, "Nobody is satisfied with the amount of money they have. There is always a desire for more." One of the workers overheard him and responded, "If I had one hundred dollars right now, I would be satisfied."

Supervisor: You think a hundred dollars will make you satisfied, now?

Worker: Oh yes, I will be cool with that.

Manager: (Whispering to the Supervisor) Watch what will happen.
Because you are a good worker, here's a hundred dollars.

Worker: Oh, thank you boss. (He stepped aside and said) My God! Why didn't I say two hundred dollars?

Manager: Supervisor, did you hear him? Everybody wants more.

King David's Desire

"One thing I have desired of the Lord, That will I seek: That I may dwell in the house of the Lord All the days of my life, to behold the beauty of the Lord, And to inquire in His temple" (Psalm 27:4).

King David was saying something very powerful here, from the core of his being. David was the guy who was at the backside of the desert as a shepherd boy, but then:

    a) He became a national hero after killing Goliath
    b) He married King Saul's daughter
    c) His family was freed from all taxes in Israel
    d) He became the King, who had everything.

David did not come from a line of monarchs, but by divine elevation he became the King of all Israel, a man who had everything life could offer, even beyond his imaginable dreams.

What does someone who has everything need? David said, "One thing I desire."

- Not two things I think about
- Not four things I wish for
- Not seven things I am planning for
- **But one thing I desire and think about**

A desire is different from a wish list.

What is a desire?

A desire is a longing, craving or yearning for. An earnest wishing for something specific.

When you crave or yearn for something, it absolutely consumes your entire being. Furthermore, it captures your focus and becomes the paramount object you think about daily.

> "Therefore I say to you, whatever things you ask when you pray, believe that you receive them, and you will have them" (Mark 11:24).

Notice what this scripture is saying here; it is not enough just to have a desire, you should pray about your desire. Your desire depends on your prayer for its fulfillment.

Your desire depends on your prayer.

David's One Desire

"One thing I desire of the Lord ... to behold the beauty of the Lord..." What does it mean to behold the beauty of the Lord? The beauty of the Lord here means WORSHIP!

What David was saying here was that God would grant him the desire to be a WORSHIPER. He was requesting that from that point on, anytime he stepped into the sanctuary, he wanted worship to spring out of his inner being to the Most High God. Not a one-time special experience.

- *Worship is incense in the nostrils of God*

- *Worship elevates His majesty and deity*

- *Worship then becomes a weapon*

- *Worship removes stress and depression from your life*

As a matter of fact, one of the greatest people God is looking for are WORSHIPERS (John 4:23-24).

You were made to "Worship Him."

Purpose of God's House

What is your purpose and motive when you step into God's house? Think about it deeply.

Many preachers step into God's house just to speak to the people. They stay in their office during prayer, praise and worship time, and after that come and give their sermon presentation.

If you are a preacher or a church leader, listen carefully. God wants you to be a worshiper because your strength as a child of God resides in your worship.

Your Strength Resides in Your Worship

> "But the hour is coming, and now is, when the true worshipers will worship the Father in spirit and truth; for the Father is seeking such to worship Him" (John 4:23).

We are not talking about one or two unique experiences of worship – No! We are talking about worship as an attitude or a lifestyle. In fact, worship should become part of your make up, not something you do once in a while.

You see, to become something is different from being something. To become rich is easier than to be wealthy. You may ask what I am talking about. Listen carefully, you may win the lottery and instantly become rich. You could also receive your family inheritance and unexpectedly become rich. But, to be "wealthy" means to remain at the same pace or level of prosperity for many years.

To Become Rich is Easier than to Be Wealthy!

King David was not talking about an unexpected experience of worship – No! Rather, a daily behavior that will eventually become your attitude, so that your attitude may become your lifestyle.

Let your desire for worship increase daily, meaning that you will always want more of God, just like the worker who asked for one hundred dollars and right after wished he had asked for two hundred dollars. As the manager said, everybody has a desire for more.

God Cannot Do Everything

Have you heard the phrase, "God can do everything"? Well, it is not quite true. When you say everything, it means – everything! You may ask, "What are you saying? The all-powerful God cannot do everything?" Absolutely Yes! God cannot do everything!

God Cannot Do Everything

There are some things God cannot do …

- a) God cannot lie – Numbers 23:19
- b) God cannot sin – 1 John 1:5
- c) God cannot tempt you with evil – James 1:13-14
- d) God cannot sleep or slumber – Psalm 121:4
- e) God cannot worship Himself – John 4:23

These are just a few examples mentioned here in the Bible. These examples tell us that God cannot do everything.

- What is your one desire on earth today?
- What is that thing you crave for, and your heart yearns for?

- You may have a house, but not a home.
- You may be successful, but not satisfied.
- You may have money, but money now controls you.
- You may have food and drink in abundance, but might not have an appetite for them.

After killing General Goliath, David became a great conqueror. After King Saul died, David became King. He had everything life could offer him, but the "one thing he lacked" was a lifestyle of a worshiper.

If your desire is based only on physical things, your desire may one day become disastrous.

May your desires not become disastrous.

Your desires for physical or material things may come, but will not last. When your desires are for spiritual things or virtues like King David, who wanted to have the lifestyle of a worshiper, you will become a victor and not a victim.

May the one thing you desire be a spiritual virtue, because worshipers always behold the beauty or the glory of the Lord.

Life Application

Identify the lack of worship in your life, and ask the Lord to give you a heart of a worshiper, or else it could be the "one thing you lack" in excelling in your walk with God.

Chapter Four

<u>One Thing I Do</u>

The one thing you maybe lacking, could be "one thing" you must do, or incorporate into your life. Doing something has to be the act of one's free and strong will.

To do means:

- To perform as an action
- To finish or complete
- To deal with or take care of

We are not talking about planning to do, have a feeling of doing, visualizing what you may be doing, or wishing you could do something – NO!

Rather, it is taking a drastic step towards the issue and performing it. To do something, there has to be an acceptance of the idea from the very core of your being. Nevertheless, the enemy of your future could be the reflections on your past. Therefore, to embrace the future, you must bury the past.

> *To embrace the Future*
>
> *You must bury the Past*

Bury The Past

> "Do not remember the former things, nor consider the things of old. Behold, I will do a new thing, now it shall spring forth..." (Isaiah 43:18-19).

When you look at this Scripture carefully, you will notice that the Bible did not specify which things of old you should not consider. So I would like to throw light on the positive and negative things from our past.

There were things that caused some of us to become victims and other things which brought us some victories in life, but let's consider the victims first.

Victims

Most of us have been victims in our past. Some of us could have been under the iron-hand treatment of our parents, wrong association at school or during college days, and/or bad friendships within the work force, abusive treatment in marriages, mental abuse or sexual abuse when we were kids or even adolescents.

No matter what you have been through, or have experienced and labeled as victimization, don't let it bury you, instead you can bury it. One thing you must do to break loose from this mental state of victimization, is to stop discussing what you want others to forget.

Stop discussing what you want others to FORGET.

Anything concerning your life prior to yesterday is dead. And if it is dead, just bury it.

God is saying, "Don't consider the things of old," meaning you must not keep reflecting on the pain of the past over and over again. Rather, think and focus on this …

"Behold, I will do a new thing, now it will spring forth." God is about to open a new chapter in your life.

Question: How will new things spring forth for you?
Answer: By forgetting the pain of the past.

The more you think about it, and talk about it, is like you are throwing a pity-party that you want others to join in to scratch or resurface the pain of your past.

You are not in a PIT to be pitied.

Stop being sorry for yourself, at this present time, by saying …

> "I would have…I could have…I should have done things differently back then."

You cannot turn back the clock. Know that, as long as it is your past, it is dead. And, if it is dead – just bury it.

If it is dead just – BURY IT!

You can't say you want to move forward, while holding on to past issues, at the same time. It will stretch you and tear you apart. You have to let one go in order to grab onto the other.

Thoughts and memories of victimization or past failures could paralyze your present life. One thing you must do is move forward to celebrate the gift of life today. As you put the past to bed, develop a strong mental mind-set which is a master key to step into the arena of confidence and conquering, because, where you stand mentally determines what grows inside you.

> *Your mental position determines*
>
> *what grows inside you.*

Victories

"For whatever is born of God overcomes the world. And this is the victory that has overcome the world—our faith" (1 John 5:4).

The happiness of victory is great, and every victory in your life needs to be celebrated. After the celebration of your victory, move on to your next assignment, because the joy of victory could embalm you. Don't let your victories of the past, cause you to become dogmatic. That is called rejoicing in past glories.

I remember after the launching of my first book, "Brokenness," the joy of finishing that project was great. One day I was visiting another church to preach and one of the members met me outside and she looked me straight in the eye and said, "Dr. Stephen, your book is so great. It has changed my entire life. Please, kindly write another book." When she said, "Please write another book," immediately I realized the joy and the celebration of that victory was over, and I had to envision new steps and look forward towards my next assignment.

Every year comes with new opportunities and new challenges. Thank God this is my fifth book. You must envision breaking new grounds and winning new territories. Don't let the victory of yesterday embalm you.

Stop rejoicing in Past Glories

One thing must be done. Stop rejoicing in past glories and focus on your next assignment because you were not made for destination. You were made for movement. "For in him we live and <u>move</u> and have our being..." (Acts. 17:28).

One Thing Apostle Paul Did

"Brethren, I do not count myself to have apprehended; **but one thing I do**, forgetting those things which are behind and reaching forward to those things which are ahead, I press toward the goal for the prize of the upward call of God in Christ Jesus" (Philippians 3:13-14).

What Are You Doing Now?

Don't try to do too many things at one time. Have you heard the phrase, *"Jack of all trades and master of none"*?

The unfortunate problem is that, when you try to do too many things you will not be effective in any. That is because your energy will be divided and your focus will be broken. What will happen is:

- *You will be stressed out*

- *You will burn out*

- *You will break down*

There could be many things you are doing today to enhance your life, better your skills, or prepare you for the next stage of excellence like:

- Exercising for your Body
- Educating yourself on some principles
- Equipping your Spirit on some spiritual truths

But don't jam yourself with too many things at one time. Kindly listen to wisdom ... do one thing at one time. When you are successful you can move to the next one.

Question: Why am I emphasizing on this so strongly?

Answer: Because God could have created the whole world in one day, but He didn't do that. Rather, he did one thing at a time. After His success he moved to the next thing on the agenda.

Do One Thing At A Time!

> "God called the light Day, and the darkness He called Night. So the evening and the morning were the first day" (Genesis 1:5).
>
> "And God called the firmament Heaven. So the evening and the morning were the second day" (Genesis 1:8).

The concept and strategy for creativity is to do one thing at a time. When you are successful in one, then you focus your energy towards the next one.

Before the Apostle Paul penned these profound words, he had previously been victimized as well as experienced some great victories.

But notice what he said, "...**one thing I do**, forgetting those things which are behind ... and I press toward the mark for the prize..." (Philippians 3:13-14).

Don't Combine Many Things Like ...

- I want to start my own company
- I want to go to school
- I want to marry while I am looking for a job
- I want to travel overseas

Don't do that!

Rather, take your time, do one thing at a time. When you succeed, then you embark on the next one.

Also, set a personal goal for your life.

Goal Setting

Goal setting must be:

Manageable – Not too high to achieve

Measurable – Duration, not too short to struggle with

Meaningful – Make sense to your purpose

Life is not a hundred meter race, rather it is a – Marathon. Furthermore, you are not in a competition with anyone. Press toward **your goal**, not the **goal of others**.

> *Press towards your goal*
>
> *Not the goal of others.*

Pressing Forward

Question: What are you pressing toward?

Paul, after **doing his one thing**, which was forgetting his:
- Tears
- Turmoil
- Tragedies
- Triumphs

He pressed forward to apprehend that which had apprehended him.

He pressed so hard, and so strong, that he caught Christ who had previously caught him on the Damascus Road. The anointing that was rubbed on him, gave him (Paul) the enablement to turn the Roman Empire upside down. The energy to press forward is already inside you. I repeat my question, what are you pressing toward today?

- *Have you lost your business? – Press forward*

- *Have you lost your parents? – Press forward*

- *Have you filed for bankruptcy? – Press forward*

- *Have you been diagnosed with cancer or AIDS – Press forward*

- *Has your marriage collapsed – Press forward*

Why? Because your best days are still ahead of you.

How many years do you have ahead of you?

With the exception of one of the following:

1. Accident or tragedy - car, ship, bike, or plane crash
2. Human Error - over-eating, no exercise, lack of rest, etc.
3. Demonic Attack - to stop or destroy your assignment

- you could live long and fulfill your purpose on earth.

I heard a preacher saying we shall live for only seventy or eighty years and die – Is it true? No, WRONG!

I said to myself, God did not say that - don't put words in His mouth. It was King David who said that, in one of his poetical expressions in the Psalms.

> "The days of our lives are seventy years; and if by reason of strength they shall be eighty years" (Psalm 90:10).

Nevertheless, this is what God said...

> "And the Lord (Elohim) said, 'My spirit shall not strive with man forever, for he is indeed flesh; yet his days shall be one hundred and twenty years'" (Genesis 6:3).

I don't know how old or young you are, but the point is, there are many days and years ahead of you. Therefore, press forward and do not limit yourself today because the best is yet to come.

David said – 70 years, but God said – 120 years

Because there are many years ahead of you, there is a champion in you to run that race. Therefore, let the champion who is asleep within you arise for the task ahead.

What Champions Do

Champions are not made in the public eye. Champions are made in secret. To be known by everyone doesn't matter so much. What matters is you discovering yourself. When you discover yourself, you will know that you are a champion in the making, because discovering yourself will bring you recovery.

Paul the Apostle discovered that
- He never saw Jesus with his physical eyes
- He was not part of the selected twelve Apostles

Yet, he pressed forward one day at a time, and he became one of the greatest champions of the Gospel.

> *What champions do everyday,*
>
> *ordinary people do*
>
> *once in a while.*

- He planted churches all over Asia Minor.
- He trained successors, to succeed him effectively.
- He wrote fourteen books of the Bible, including Hebrews.

Again, the "one thing" that Apostle Paul did was to forget his:

a) Painful past
b) Pitfalls
c) Persecutions
d) Praise of prosperity

But, he moved forward towards the high calling of God.

What about you, reading this book?

When you discover that the potential to be a champion is asleep in you, you will recover from all kinds of setbacks.

Again, be excited about the gift of life today.

- *Now you know you can live for a long time to accomplish your purpose.*

- *Now you know there is a champion asleep in you.*

- *Now you know you should do one thing at a time.*

Now, therefore, let the champion in you arise, breakout from any form of human limitations. Let diligence and consistency be your secret and the champion in you shall be released into motion.

Congratulations, champion, you have made it.

> *Let the*
>
> *Champion in you*
>
> *Arise!*

Life Application

Identify your past achievements, and celebrate them. After celebrating, stop rejoicing in past glories and ask the Lord for the enablement to do more for his Kingdom, or else it will be the "one thing" that could hinder you in life.

Chapter Five

One Thing Is Needed

Mr. Friztgero always got to his office at 8:00 a.m. everyday for the past five years, but on September 11, 2001 he drew a demarcation line between **want** and **need**, and the outcome was unbelievable. He wanted to be at work at exactly 8:00 a.m. but there was a need in his child's life and he wanted to respond to it.

The need was to take his son to the first day of his grade school. He knew it would help the confidence and the psyche of his son. He also wanted to be at work in the ninety-story building at the World Trade Center in New York City at exactly 8:00 a.m.

Nevertheless, he responded to the "one thing" that was needed, and it did not only save his live, but changed his destiny forever.

> ## *The One Thing That Is Needed*
> ## *Always Changes Our Destiny*

After dropping off his son and leaving the first grade school, he rushed to his office at the World Trade Center reaching at 8:55 a.m. The first building was on fire. While he watched right there in disbelief, the second building was hit by an airplane. After that horrible and devastating day, his entire company of seventy-five (75) workers had perished as the whole building collapsed into ashes.

The "one thing that was needed," saved his life from death, because he should have been in the building at that specific time. A **need** is different from a **want**.

There could be many things you want to picture yourself possessing, parading around you, or experiencing in this life. But what you **need** is far more important than what you **want**.

> ## *What you need is far more important*
> ## *than what you want.*

The Wants of Life

When a lady steps into a shopping mall, it appears that she wants everything in that shopping mall; the clothes, the shoes and the new designs etc. Sometimes she will buy things that look beautiful but after reaching home, she may say, "Why did I buy these?"

- A want always appeals to the eye.
- A want makes you feel good.
- A need makes you feel satisfied.
- A need solves a present problem.

Likewise, when a man steps into a car showroom looking at the cars; the new models, different colors, etc. his knees will begin to knock against each other, the palms of his hands begin to sweat, he want this, he wants that, and he can't take his eyes off them.

Nevertheless, the "one that is needed" is the one that his pocket can afford. The **wants** of life are enormous and staggering.

If I may ask you - what do you need in life?

When you start to think about this question, maybe your mind will go blank, and then you will regroup your thoughts before you can say something substantial. Perhaps what you <u>need</u> and what you <u>want</u> has been <u>mixed together in a wrong way</u>.

God – does not need You to be – God

a) God doesn't need you to be God.
b) When you worship God you are not doing Him a favor – Not at all!
c) When you worship Christ, you do yourself a favor.
d) You can't vote God into power, and you can't vote Him out of power

> "God, who made the world and everything in it, since He is Lord of heaven and earth, does not dwell in temples made with hands. Nor is He worshiped with men's hands, as though He needed anything, since He gives to all life, breath, and all things" (Acts 17:24-25).

Notice what the Bible says, "As though he needed anything," meaning God doesn't need anything from you to make him God.

Without you serving him, or devoting your life to him, it doesn't weaken his power or ability to function as God or demote him from his throne – No! Not at all. But you need God to function or operate in life.

Why do you need God?

> "... Since He gives to **all life**, breath, and all things" (Acts 17:25).

Therefore, the very breath in your nostrils and the functioning of your organs come from Him. This means you need God to exist, to function, and to fulfill your purpose on earth.

Serving God or devoting your life to him is the greatest privilege you have in life. You are doing yourself a favor by serving the Lord, while he gives you what it takes for you to fulfill your purpose here on earth.

The Product always needs the – Manufacturer.
The manufacturer could do away with any product and come with another product.

The Manufacturer Makes His Product Fulfill Its Purpose.

One Thing you have to Understand is That …

- Mankind on this earth – exists
- Planets in the universe – exist
- Animals in the jungle – exist
- Fish in the sea and the ocean – exist
- Birds in the Atmosphere – exist

God is the being from which <u>all existence comes from</u>.

Therefore, if you don't know Jesus as your Lord and personal savior, please stop here, and go to the end of this book "Decision to accept Christ," and pray that prayer right away, and give your heart to Jesus Christ. Something miraculous will happen to you today!

Mary's Choice

Notice this powerful scripture below.

> "Now it happened as they went that He entered a certain village; and a certain woman named Martha welcomed Him into her house. And she had a sister called Mary, who also **sat at Jesus' feet and heard His word**" (Luke 10:38-39).

> "And Jesus answered and said to her, "Martha, Martha, you are worried and troubled about **many things**" But one thing is needed, and Mary has chosen that good part which will not be taken away from her" (Luke 10:41-42).

Martha welcomed Jesus into her house. Right away, she started cooking for Jesus. Martha became frustrated carrying the workload alone. Martha said to Jesus, "Let Mary come to the kitchen and help me with the cooking."

Jesus replied, "No!"

"Martha, Martha, you **trouble yourself** with many things."

"But **one thing is needed,** and Mary has chosen that."

The amazing fact about Jesus is that…

You should not cook for Jesus if he hasn't asked you to.

- He may be already full
- He may be fasting

- He may not be hungry
- He may not have an appetite for food at that time

Martha might have been cooking without Jesus' knowledge. That's why he said, "You **trouble yourself about many things**. But one thing is needed, and Mary has chosen that."

What is the one thing needed?

To sit under the feet of Jesus and listen to his Word, take advantage of his visit and receive from God. A man's word reveals his philosophy.

Profound words could change your entire life. People may leave you, but their words will not leave you. Positive words prepare you to fight on.

People May Leave You - But Their Words Will Not Leave You.

Martha didn't like Jesus' response. Sometimes what you **want to hear** may be different from what you **need to hear**. Martha did not learn the lesson from Jesus' correction. Therefore, her attitude never changed.

After Lazarus was raised from the dead and Jesus visited their house, guess what?

Martha was in the kitchen cooking again. After that visit, we never heard about Martha anywhere again in the Bible.

Now, before Jesus raised Lazarus up from the dead, this dialogue took place between Jesus and Martha.

Jesus:	Your brother will live again.
Martha:	Yes, I know.
Jesus:	I am the resurrection and the life.
Martha:	Yes, I know.
Jesus:	Now, take away the stone.
Martha:	No way, right now he is rotten.
Jesus:	Did I not say to you, "If you believe, you shall see the glory of God?"

Martha said, "I know, I know and I know," as is the custom of some people. But she didn't know anything, because she never sat at Jesus' feet and she didn't have **the Word in her life**.

One thing she needed was the Word of Christ in her life.

- Martha was not strong in the Lord.

- Martha was not rooted and grounded in the Word.

- Martha was not stable or firm in Christ's teachings.

What do you need?

What you need may not be – Money

What you need may not be – Beautiful Homes

What you need may not be – Jewelry

What you need may not be – An Expensive Car

What you need is the divine Word of God

These positive and seasonal words can sustain you in the time of turmoil.

> "Heaven and earth will pass away, but My words will by no means pass away" (Matthew 24:35).

What you need solves a problem

What you need sustains you

> "But Mary stood outside by the tomb weeping, and as she wept she stooped down and looked into the tomb. Jesus said to her, 'Mary!' She turned and said to Him, 'Rabboni!' (which is to say, Teacher)" (John 20:11, 16).

Mary, who, on the other hand, sat at Jesus' feet to hear his Word and allowed the word to sink within her, became strong, stable and immovable in her faith. We have heard about this Mary on several occasions.

Even after the death of Jesus, one writer said that all the other ladies left the cemetery, but Mary was still standing there searching for her Master. She was the first person Jesus revealed himself to after the resurrection.

When Opportunity Knocks

When you knock at the door of this world, it will be silent but don't give up, keep on knocking. Nevertheless, when opportunity comes knocking, open the door without any hesitation.

What you **need**, might just be, behind that door.

Apply this to your own life.

Life Application

Identify the fact that you need to incorporate the Word of God in your own life daily to become strong as you sit at Jesus' feet.

Chapter Six

<u>One Thing You Lack</u>

Every human being on planet earth lacks one thing or another, whether in character, behavior or mannerism, no matter who you are or your educational background, your financial position, the anointing on your life or political affiliation. There is always something or "one thing" that could make you better.

I think it is part of the very core of our being, the fragile or weakest part of our being. This is why we hear phrases like:
- No one is perfect.
- To err is human, to forgive is divine.
- Everyone makes mistakes.

My objective in this book is to help you to do the following:

1) Locate that "one thing you lack" (positive or negative)
2) Identify it
3) Deal with it before it messes you up
4) Don't let it destroy your very destiny

Moses spoke face-to-face with God. He was anointed with fresh oil from on high. He became the deliverer and the savior of the Children of Israel. He wrought incredible and unusual miracles. He opened the Red Sea with his shepherd's staff.

But the "one thing he lacked" was getting a handle on his <u>anger problem</u>. He never reached where God had destined him to reach because of the "one thing he lacked" in his life – anger control.

Never overlook or underestimate that "one thing you lack," because it could make or break you.

<u>The Rich Young Ruler</u>

A rich young man heard of Jesus and started running after him. When he got there, he knelt before him asking him how to get eternal life. Let us analyze what took place during that encounter in the Bible.

> "Now as He was going out on the road, one came running, knelt before Him, and asked Him, 'Good Teacher, what shall I do that I may inherit eternal life?' So Jesus said to him, 'Why do you call Me good? No one is good but One, that is, God. You know the commandments: 'Do not commit adultery,' 'Do not murder,' 'Do not steal,' 'Do not bear false witness,' 'Do not defraud,' 'Honor your father and your mother.'' And he answered and said to Him, 'Teacher, all these things I have kept from my youth.' Then Jesus, looking at him, loved him, and said to him, '<u>One thing you lack</u>: Go your way, sell whatever you have and give to the poor, and you will have treasure in heaven; and come, take up the

cross, and follow Me.' But he was sad at this word, and went away sorrowful, for he had great possessions" (Mark 10:17-22).

There are many things you could do in your life to excel, but you still may not succeed until you do one specific or significant thing that will catapult you into prominence.

Mr. Ross Perot, the Texas millionaire and a one time American presidential candidate once said, "You need only one good idea to make you live like a king."

Before we come to the "one thing" the rich young ruler lacked, let us take a step back and analyze the three things the rich man did.

    1) He ran after Jesus
    2) He knelt down before him
    3) He asked what he could do to get eternal life

He ran after Jesus

Rich people don't normally run, except the ones who want to exercise their bodies. In the days of the Bible, rich people often sent their servants to do their bidding for them. They walked gorgeously with their chests out, because of the things they possessed. This rich man ran after Jesus, and when he got to him he did not say anything right away, but surprisingly, he knelt down before him.

He Knelt Down

Rich people don't normally kneel down before anyone. Kneeling down in those days signified the lowest state of a person, and was normally done by poor people. Many rich people refuse to kneel down before anyone because of their pride and prestige. They will only be willing to do so when their life is on the line. This rich man knelt before Jesus and he asked the unbelievable question.

Eternal Life

"What shall I do to inherit eternal life?" the rich man asked Jesus.

Let us diagnose how to get eternal life.

There are three kinds of life:

1) Physical life
2) Spiritual life
3) Eternal life

Physical life plus (+) Spiritual life

= Eternal life

Physical life minus (-) Spiritual life

= Eternal death

Notice this, eternal life does not begin when you die and go to heaven – NO! Eternal life begins here on earth when you accept the spiritual life that Jesus offers by being born-again into the family of Christ. Eternal life is added to your physical and spiritual life and, right away, you begin your journey of eternal life here, before you enter into glory.

Jesus told the young rich man to go and observe the Mosaic Laws and he replied that he had observed them from his youth. Jesus then looked him straight in the eye and loved him, knowing that he was an honest man who had observed the Law to the fullest.

Jesus then told him the one thing he lacked was to go and **sell** whatever he had and **give** them to the poor. He would then have treasure in heaven, and then he should take up his cross and **follow** him. The young man was saddened by what Jesus said and went away upset, because he had great possessions.

Misunderstood

The rich man ran to Jesus, knelt before him, and asked for eternal life, of his own choice, but he misunderstood everything the Master said to him. He thought that Jesus wanted him to go broke or poor.

Even today, many believers who read this portion of the scripture still misinterpret it.

There are three major object lessons in what Jesus said.

1) **Sell**
2) **Give**
3) **Come, Follow Me**

What do you think of what Jesus said, and how do you understand it? Open your spirit as we dig deep into it.

Sell   Nobody gets into buying and selling and expects to lose money. No! When you make that decision, I believe your expectation is to make more money, right? Jesus wanted this rich man to get involved in selling or investment in order to make more money, but he misunderstood him.

Give   "He who has pity on the poor lends to the Lord, And He will pay back what he has given" (Proverbs 19:17).
"Give, and it will be given to you..." (Luke 6:38).

The above Scriptures show that when you give, you don't throw your money away, but rather you position yourself to get more back. This rich man didn't understand that.

Come   All those to whom Jesus extended a *Follow Me* personal invitation later became Apostles. The rich man missed an

Apostolic calling. In fact, Jesus wanted this man to move from just being rich to becoming a millionaire, but he misunderstood and left sad.

"The entrance of Your words gives light; It gives understanding to the simple" (Psalm 119:130).

Mistakes

"But he was sad at this word, and went away sorrowful, for he had great possessions" (Mark 10:22).

He did not only misunderstand Jesus, but he also made the mistake of leaving the presence of Christ sad without asking any questions. Don't forget that he came to Jesus running, and when he got there, he knelt before him in submission asking for eternal life.

Jesus gave him his undivided attention, yet he left his presence with a moody attitude. Never leave God's presence with sadness or anger.

"He who is slow to anger is better than the mighty, and he who rules his spirit than he who takes a city" (Proverbs 16:32).

Money

Check This Out

This rich man had:
- Observed the Laws of Moses from his youthful days

- Become rich
- Needed eternal life
- <u>Been taught</u> by Jesus what to do
- Left Jesus' presence sad and angry

This man wanted to serve God minus his money! The scripture says Jesus looked at him and loved him. I believe Jesus knew he was telling the truth, otherwise Jesus would have told him he was lying.

Is it possible to live a righteous life? Yes! Even Paul said in Philippians 3:6, concerning righteousness, which was in the law, he was blameless.

This man was ready to serve in the temple – he was living a holy life, but he was not ready to put his money at the feet of the Lord to worship him.

Unfortunately, many believers today are just like this rich man. You may be willing to worship the Lord in His house in the following capacities:

- Holy living
- Fasting and prayer
- Playing musical instruments
- Singing in the choir
- Evangelism, intercessory ministries
- Men, women, youth and children's ministries
- Functioning in leadership positions

But, you are not ready to serve him with your tithe, offering or anything concerning your MONEY. The

Lord said it will be hard for such ones to enter into the Kingdom of Heaven.

The Bible refers to this man as a RICH MAN. He was a stingy person. He had a grip on his money, so much that his money had enslaved him. When it came to the choice between God and money, he chose **money**.

Some people normally say they need only to worship God with their heart. Wrong!

- Money is the cream of your life
- Money is the sweat of your toil
- Money represents your strength

Until you can lay some of your money at the feet of the Lord, there is a stronghold on your life.

Money is part of your worship to God.

Two Masters

If I may ask you, what are the two masters that rule the world? You may believe the two masters who rule or dominate the world are God and Satan. If so, sorry, you are wrong!

Notice this scripture carefully.

> "No one can serve two masters; for either he will hate the one and love the other, or else he will be loyal to the one and despise the other. You cannot serve God and mammon" (Matthew 6:24).

Jesus was speaking to His disciples and declared to them that the two masters in this world are <u>not</u>
- a)   The power of God, or
- b)   The power of Satan – not at all.

As a believer, Satan is already defeated and he is not your master. Rather it is this:
- a)   God as a Master, or
- b)   Mammon (money) as a master.

"Mammon" is the old Aramaic word for money. Child of God, as we have seen, the two masters that rule this world are <u>God</u> and <u>money</u>.

> ### *The two masters who rule this world are*
> ### *God and Money*

Money is a strong master. If you don't master it, it certainly will master you. Apparently, this rich man had been mastered by his money and found it difficult to submit to the possessor of the universe.

- Where do you stand?
- Has your money got a grip on you?
- Are you stingy?
- Do you want to serve God minus your money?

One of the rich man's problems was that he wanted to serve God but not with his money.

> *This rich man loved God.*
>
> *He wanted to serve God,*
>
> *But the "one thing he lacked"*
>
> *was the "Spirit of Generosity."*

Generosity, or the willingness to give, was a missing ingredient in this rich man's life, and because of that, he lost eternal life.

What should you do from today?

a)   Identify the "one specific thing you lack."
b)   Locate that one thing – make it crystal clear.
c)   Begin to deal with it.

If you do not take these steps the "one thing you lack" could lead you into trouble, and eventually it will lead you to a dead end.

If you identify the "one thing you lack" and begin to deal with it, your life will be a success story.

Apply this to your own life.

Life Application

Identify **stinginess** and the grip that money has on your own life or else, no matter how you serve God, Money shall be your master.

Pray for the "Spirit of Generosity" or the willingness to give towards God's work, for without this money could affect your eternal life.

Chapter Seven

<u>What This Prince Lacked</u>

"You are a Prince automatically when you are born from the line of a King or a Monarch."

There is one school of thought that says that leaders are BORN.

Another school of thought says that leaders are MADE.

Nevertheless, when children are born to a King or a Queen, who are expected to inherit the throne as future leaders or Kings, they are assigned to Elders or leaders, and even professionals who train them from childhood.

They are trained on issues of Life, Leadership, Law, Lawlessness and Love.

Together with their training they are taught on:
   a) Ethics
   b) Morality
   c) Protocol and
   d) Issues regarding Conduct and Behavior.

> "Sons were born to David in Hebron: His firstborn was Amnon by Ahinoam the Jezreelitess; his second, Chileab, by Abigail the widow of Nabal the Carmelite; the third, Absalom the son of Maacah, the daughter of Talmai, king of Geshur; the fourth, Adonijah the son of Haggith; the fifth, Shephatiah the son of Abital; and the sixth, Ithream, by David's wife Eglah. These were born to David in Hebron" (2 Samuel 3:2-5).

The two sons or Princes of King David that are well known, according to these verses may be "Absalom" and "Adonijah." Regardless of his training and the education that was given to him as a Prince of the Kingdom, Absalom could not conform to the Princely image the elders and professionals tried so hard to patiently mold him into.

Absalom did not only lack one thing, rather this Prince lacked many things.

Absalom had:
- Personal problems
- Attitude problems
- Problems in the Kingdom
- Resentment against the King

These are what I call "Self-defeating habits." Notice what happened in these verses.

> "After this Absalom the son of David had a lovely sister, whose name was Tamar; and Amnon the son of David loved her. Amnon was so distressed over his sister Tamar that he became sick; for she was a virgin. And it was improper for Amnon to do anything to her. However, he would not heed her

voice; and being stronger than she, he forced her and lay with her" (2 Samuel 13:1-2, 14).

Amnon, one of the Princes, had just raped his half-sister called Tamar. Now, this issue became a big problem in the family.

Unfortunately, this problem led to conflict and the conflict led to a CRISIS.

> "And it came to pass, after two full years, that Absalom had sheepshearers in Baal Hazor, which is near Ephraim; so Absalom invited all the king's sons" (2 Samuel 13:23).

After the horrible incident of Amnon raping his own sister, the entire family was devastated.

- King David was Angry
- Prince Absalom was Furious
- The whole family was Outraged

The Bible was silent about the steps King David took regarding this horrible incident of incest that affected the Royal family.

Prince Absalom, on the other hand, was so furious with his brother Amnon's behavior that, for two years he could not forgive him, instead, his anger led to hatred and he devised a plan to kill his own brother. Absalom was filled with so much hatred and resentment that he killed his own brother in cold blood.

> *Absalom was filled with*
> *HATRED AND RESENTMENT.*
> *What this Prince lacked was*
> *FORGIVENESS AND FORBEARANCE.*

Absalom did not only lack one thing, not at all!

He lacked many virtues as a Prince. And it led him into exile in the country of Syria, in the city of Geshur.

Furthermore, after Prince Absalom returned from Syria, you might assume he had learned his lesson and worked on his character.

But this Prince still lacked discernment about how to operate in the Kingdom. The next move from Absalom was to undermine his own father's throne and his Kingdom.

> "Moreover Absalom would say, "Oh, that I were made judge in the land, and everyone who has any suit or cause would come to me; then I would give him justice." And so it was, whenever anyone came near to bow down to him, that he would put out his hand and take him and kiss him. In this manner Absalom acted toward all Israel who came to the king for judgment. So Absalom stole the hearts of the men of Israel" (2 Samuel 15:4-6).

Instead of this Prince becoming a tool to UNDERGIRD his father's Kingdom, he became a weapon to UNDERMINE him.

Don't UNDERMINE Your Leaders.

UNDERGIRD Them.

Notice the following skills and abilities of Absalom:

- Style
- Strategy
- Strength

Absalom used psychology and deception to steal the heart of all Israel. He began to rally people around himself to dethrone his own father, in order to establish his own Kingdom.

Prince Absalom was ROYALTY

But he lacked LOYALTY!

This Prince knew how to mobilize and motivate the elders and other subjects in the Kingdom toward a specific goal. Instead of using these skills to enhance and under gird his father's Kingdom, he flowed in the opposite direction, which eventually led to a dead end.

Finally, Prince Absalom tried to make himself King in Hebron. And because there cannot be two kings in one Kingdom, the battle for the throne began right away.

From the get-go, Prince Absalom seemed to have the support from the crowd. Even some trusted key leaders like Ahitophel and Hushai left King David's camp to join Prince Absalom.

Looking at the atmosphere and the momentum booming in his camp, Prince Absalom thought there was going to be a BREAKTHROUGH. Little did he know that a breakthrough can turn into a BREAKDOWN.

Be careful!

Your BREAKTHROUGH

can become a BREAKDOWN.

"For the battle there was scattered over the face of the whole countryside, and the woods devoured more people that day than the sword devoured. Then Absalom met the servants of David. Absalom rode on a mule. The mule went under the thick boughs of a great terebinth tree, and his head caught in the terebinth; so he was left hanging between heaven and earth. And the mule which was under him went on. Now a certain man saw it and told Joab, and said, "I just saw Absalom hanging in a terebinth tree!" Then Joab said, "I cannot linger with you." And he took three spears in his hand and thrust them through Absalom's heart, while he was still alive in the midst of the terebinth tree. And ten young men who bore Joab's armor surrounded Absalom, and struck and killed him. So Joab blew the trumpet, and the people returned from pursuing Israel. For Joab held back the people. And they took Absalom and cast him into a large pit in the woods, and laid a very large heap of stones over him. Then all Israel fled, everyone to his tent" (2 Samuel 18:8-10, 14-17).

Absalom's jealousy and selfish ambition to become King drove him to fight his own father in his quest to dethrone, and possibly kill him. Absalom had people's approval, but what this Prince lacked was God's approval.

> *Absalom had people's*
>
> *APPROVAL*
>
> *What this Prince lacked was*
>
> *God's APPROVAL!*

Prince Absalom died like a dog, and his body was thrown away like an animal's carcass.

The Bible was clear when it said:

> "There is a way that seems right to a man, but its end is the way of death" (Proverbs 16:25).

Absalom's character and lifestyle as a Prince in the Bible should not be seen as an isolated incident, but also a figurative example. Therefore, I believe we can extract some life application and illustration from this Prince.

The Believer As A Prince

In the study of typology, we understand that King David is one of the types of Christ in the Old Testament. And the throne of David shall live forever, which is a type of the Kingdom or church of Christ. Therefore, we want to compare some of the things that happened in the Kingdom of David to what is going on today, in the Kingdom of the church of Christ Jesus.

We can say that every born-again believer is a King's Kid, and that makes you a Prince or a Princess in the Kingdom of God.

The Bible declares in 1 Peter 2:9:

> "But you are a chosen generation, a royal priesthood, a holy nation, His own special people, that you may proclaim the praises of Him who called you out of darkness into His marvelous light."

Nevertheless, the fact that you are a Prince of Princess, and maybe able to speak in tongues, does not mean that you can do anything, anyhow, in the Kingdom of God or the church, and walk away free. No way!

All of us as believers, and even church Elders, Pastors and Bishops, should understand that there are a lot of things that we lack in our own lives, character and mannerisms, as God's Princes and Princesses during this end time, just like Prince Absalom.

Morality Vs Mercy In The Ministry

What happens if someone in the church or the Kingdom of God has a moral problem? Let's say a committed member or even a leader, what should we do?

First, we should identify the problem. Secondly, we should address the problem and know what type of solution could be offered. Thirdly, if the person admits the fact that he or she has a problem, then we should do everything in our power to give this individual a helping hand.

Through prayer, fasting, deliverance ministration and even some professional help, like seeing a counselor, psychiatrist or psychotherapist. We are not called to condemn people, or kill our wounded soldiers. Rather, we are commissioned to "pour in the oil and the wine" on their wounds. Read Luke 10:30-37.

After all these spiritual and physical steps of mercy are taken, if this individual continues this lifestyle, then there is the need for discipline. Discipline should not be seen as destructive.

> ### *Discipline is not Destruction*

Where there is no discipline there is disorder. And, where there is disorder, the Holy Spirit always steps out.

Seeds of Deceit in the Church

You noticed that when Prince Absalom was not happy regarding the way his father was handling some things in the Kingdom, he started to sow seeds of deceit in the minds of the children of Israel (2 Samuel 15:1-6). And the Bible says that he stole the hearts of the people. Such action was a seed of deceit or deception that he was sowing in the Kingdom. Today, we have seen that this attitude is so rampant in the Kingdom of Christ.

When a church Deacon or even Associate Pastor is not happy about the way the Senior Pastor or Bishop is handling something in the church, right away, he or she begins to follow the footsteps of Prince Absalom.

a) Begins to call for secret meetings.
b) Organizes deceptive prayer meetings to rally people around themselves.
c) Sowing seeds of deceit against the head Pastor or Bishop.
d) Maneuvering and devising a strategy to get followers.

e) Planning to leave with some members to start his or her own church.

Wrong motives and wrong methodology end with deadly mistakes!

Many young, gifted, promising preachers started this path just like Absalom, and ended up tragically.

DON'T EVEN THINK ABOUT IT.
PLEASE DON'T DO IT!

Don't UNDERMINE

your spiritual leader. Instead,

UNDER GIRD YOUR PASTOR.

The right thing to do when you feel that you cannot sit under the leadership of your Pastor or Bishop is to go to him/her and get:

a) His/her blessing as your Spiritual leader
b) Support from the church family
c) Receive his/her wisdom for your new direction

When you are leaving any ministry or organization:

a) Don't slam the door on your way out.
b) Close the door gently.
c) One day, you may enter that same door again.

If you don't follow these steps, and you leave in the atmosphere of chaos, by dividing the church:

a) Your leader can pronounce a curse – and it may happen to you.
b) The spirit of division will follow you.
c) You may reap what you have sown in the future.

1) Noah got off track and got drunk with wine, but when he cursed Canaan, it happened (Genesis 9:20-27).

2) King Saul was being troubled by an evil spirit to kill David, but David said, "I will not touch the Lord's anointed" (1 Samuel 24: 1-6).

3) Laban cheated Jacob for twenty years, but when he vocalized a curse, it affected his own daughter (Genesis 31:25-37).

Whether your leader is living right according to Biblical principles or not, you don't have any right to sow seeds of deceit, chaos, or division in the ministry of God.

Division in the Church

What happens when confusion and division is about to strike in the church?

Just like Prince Absalom did and got Ahitophel, King David's counselor, and Hushai, on his side, what should you do?

Listen carefully to what Apostle Paul said.

> "Now I urge you, brethren, note those who cause divisions and offenses, contrary to the doctrine which you learned, and avoid them. For those who are such do not serve our Lord Jesus Christ, but their own belly, and by smooth words and flattering speech deceive the hearts of the simple" (Romans 16:17-18).

No matter the circumstances regarding the confusion which may lead to division in the church. DON'T DO IT!

Personal Experience

In 1999, I was preaching in Faith Christian Church in Wisconsin, in the United States. After the message, I made an altar call. The altar was filled with people. I asked them to raise their hands and touch the glory of God as we prayed.

Suddenly, the power of God filled the place. Many were slain under the power of God without anyone touching them, and they were all speaking in tongues, and crying under a unique visitation.

Right away, the Pastor ran to the platform and took the microphone from my hands and started shaking his head with a "no" sign. He then announced to the congregation that what was happening was not from God because he, the Pastor, didn't believe in speaking in tongues. In fact, he started begging the members to leave the sanctuary. Without receiving his tithe and offering, he closed the service.

Hundreds of members of the church were crying in the lobby because of what the Pastor did.

After this, five (5) key leaders took me out to a restaurant and apologized to me concerning what the Pastor did. I accepted their apology. Finally, they said they believed what the Pastor did was a sin against the Holy Spirit, therefore, they could not stay under his leadership.

"Tomorrow," they said, "We are going make plans to buy a building to start a new church, and we want you to be our Pastor or leader." I looked them in the eye and said, "No way, I won't do it!"

They spoke to me for hours, trying to convince me. By the way, everything they said made sense. Even some of their complaints were Biblically accurate. But, I declined their offer to be their Pastor. I told them that, obviously, there was a problem in their church and I was there to help facilitate a solution, not to divide the church of God.

They had money and their offer looked like a breakthrough, but it could have ended up as a BREAKDOWN.

> **Things that look like**
>
> **BREAKTHROUGHS**
>
> **Could turn into**
>
> **BREAKDOWNS.**

"But also for this very reason, giving all diligence, add to your faith virtue, to virtue knowledge, to knowledge self-control, to self-control perseverance, to perseverance godliness, to godliness brotherly kindness, and to brotherly kindness love. For if these things are yours and abound, you will be neither barren nor unfruitful in the knowledge of our Lord Jesus Christ. For he who lacks these things is shortsighted, even to blindness, and has forgotten that he was cleansed from his old sins" (2 Peter 1"5-9).

Apostle Paul said that if you lack these things you are blind, shortsighted and cannot see afar off.

There is an African proverb which says:

"If you begin where your grandfather ended, you will end where your grandfather begun."

Our Fathers of Faith begun their churches with two or three people and ended with hundreds. If we begin with hundreds, we will end with two or three people.

I had 99 percent of the entire congregation of four hundred people supporting me to begin a new church with them. But, I declined and said NO!

Not because I could not do it, I could do it. I may get people's approval but may lack God's approval.

> *Don't get people's*
>
> *APPROVAL*
>
> *while lacking*
>
> *GOD'S APPROVAL.*

Lack of patience and foresight, and taking advantage of broken situations could be very costly.

What you lack in your quest to do God's work might turn into a dead-end for you. Don't ever be like Prince Absalom. Because, what he lacked, literally destroyed him.

Chapter Eight

<u>What This King Lacked</u>

Saul was anointed the first King of the people of Israel. God appointed Saul to be King, not because he was qualified or deserved it. Absolutely not!

God in His infinite mercy and divine sovereignty picked Saul to be King of Israel.

> "Then Samuel took a flask of oil and poured it on his head, and kissed him and said: 'Is it not because the Lord has anointed you commander over His inheritance?'" (1 Samuel 10:1).

Samuel, the prophet, and other priests were the architects who helped King Saul to organize and structure things in his Kingdom. King Saul began to win wars over the Philistines and neighboring nations.

Samuel also functioned as the High Priest. As a High Priest, one of his duties was to perform sacrifices in the sanctuary.

The Bible says, "Where the word of a king is, there is power; and who may say to him, 'What are you doing?'" (Ecclesiastes 8:4). This indicates that position always comes with power.

But, whether you are a King or a Queen, or a person in authority, one thing you should not do is to break rank and do things you are not assigned to do.

> ### *Absolute Power*
>
> ### *Corrupts Absolutely!*

King Saul was then enjoying POWER! Pride and ego took hold of him and he began to do things he was not assigned or allowed to do.

Read 1 Samuel 13:9-13:

> "So Saul said, 'Bring a burnt offering and peace offerings here to me.' And he offered the burnt offering. Now it happened, as soon as he had finished presenting the burnt offering, that Samuel came; and Saul went out to meet him, that he might greet him. And Samuel said, 'What have you done?' And Saul said, 'When I saw that the people were scattered from me, and that you did not come within the days appointed, and that the Philistines gathered together at Michmash, then I said, 'The Philistines will now come down on me at Gilgal, and I have not made supplication to the Lord.' Therefore I felt compelled, and offered a burnt offering.' And Samuel said to Saul, 'You have done foolishly. You have not kept the commandment of the Lord your God, which He commanded you. For now the Lord would have established your kingdom over Israel forever'."

Notice what King Saul did. He stepped into the office of the Priesthood and he performed burnt and peace offerings. King Saul was not a PRIEST. And therefore, was not allowed or had no rights to perform these ceremonies.

Pride had eaten up King Saul and ego had set in when he took matters into his own hands. Saul, thinking that because he was the King, he could do anything and get away with it.

> "Pride goes before destruction, and a haughty spirit before a fall. Better to be of a humble spirit with the lowly, than to divide the spoil with the proud" (Proverbs 16:18-19).

> ***Pride always***
>
> ***creates your own Pitfalls.***

Samuel, the prophet, was honest and spoke passionately to him when he said, "You have done foolishly" (1 Samuel 13:13).

To step into the office of the Priesthood and offer burnt and peace offerings, Saul was not only wrong, he was DEAD WRONG!

All these were warning signs for Saul, hoping he would change, but he did not.

Seven (7) ways to Locate the Doorways of Pride

1) Pride comes when you think you know better than anyone else around you.

2) Pride comes when you think you look better than those around you.

3) Pride comes when you refuse to take Godly instructions from your mentors or spiritual leaders.

4) Pride can give birth to blindness of your future.

5) Pride can easily invade your heart when you are in a position of power.

6) Pride tells you to do things another way, even when specific instructions are given to you.

7) Pride always creates its own pitfalls for you.

Pride makes you overlook specific instructions.

Finally, King Saul refused to take specific instructions from the Prophet Samuel, and look how pride let him to disobedience.

"Samuel also said to Saul, 'The Lord sent me to anoint you king over His people, over Israel. Now therefore, heed the voice of the words of the Lord. Thus says the Lord of hosts: 'I will punish Amalek for what he did to Israel, how he ambushed him on the way when he came up from Egypt. Now go and attack Amalek, and utterly destroy all that they have, and do not spare them. But kill both man and woman, infant and nursing child, ox and sheep, camel and donkey'" (1 Samuel 15:1-3).

"But Saul and the people spared Agag and the best of the sheep, the oxen, the fatlings, the lambs, and all that was good, and were unwilling to utterly destroy them. But everything despised and worthless, that they utterly destroyed. Now the word of the Lord came to Samuel, saying, 'I greatly regret that I have set up Saul as king, for he has turned back from following Me, and has not performed My commandments.' And it grieved Samuel, and he cried out to the Lord all night" (1 Samuel 15:9-11).

"So Samuel said: 'Has the Lord as great delight in burnt offerings and sacrifices, as in obeying the voice of the Lord? Behold, to obey is better than sacrifice, And to heed than the fat of rams. For rebellion is as the sin of witchcraft, and stubbornness is as iniquity and idolatry. Because you have rejected the word of the Lord, He also has rejected you from being king'" (1 Samuel 15:22-23).

Notice how the Prophet ends his rebuke, "To obey is better than sacrifice." Can you imagine how one single element can cause a King to lose the following?
- His Kingdom
- His Throne

- His Position

King Saul was filled with PRIDE and EGO. He disregarded all advice and cautions from prophets and his advisors because of the "one thing he lacked," and that was the "Spirit of Humility."

King Saul was filled with

PRIDE

Because of the One Thing He Lacked –

HUMILITY!

Please, kindly extract an object lesson from King Saul's behavior and apply it to your own life.

Look at yourself in the mirror and examine your heart in regards to the seven (7) ways to locate the doorways of pride, from the previous pages. Contemplate on them deeply, so that you can clothe yourself with the "one thing" King Saul lacked, and that was Humility.

> "Likewise you younger people, submit yourselves to your elders. Yes, all of you be submissive to one another, and be clothed with humility, for "God resists the proud, but gives grace to the humble." Therefore humble yourselves under the mighty hand of God, that He may exalt you in due time" (1 Peter 5:5-6).

- Humility is a Kingdom Principle.
- God is not a respecter of Persons,

- But, God is a respecter of Principles.
- What God does for one person in Principle,
- He will also do it for you.

- Talents and skills could take you to great places and before great men.

- But, humility and character is what can keep you there.

- Humility, therefore, is a double-edged sword. It cuts everywhere, so get hold of it.

- If you "Lack this one thing," you will soon reach a DEAD END!

Chapter Nine

What These Great Men Lacked

ADAM He was created in the image of God almighty.
He had the title deed of the whole earth.
He gave names to everything in this world.
He talked face to face with God.
BUT – one thing he lacked was the "ability to correct his wife." And he lost everything (Genesis 3:4-6).

NOAH He lived a holy and righteous life.
He preached for one hundred and twenty years.
He built an ark to save his generation.
He picked two of every animal under great anointing to enter the ark for safety.
BUT – the one thing he lacked was how to "control his appetite for drinking" (Genesis 9:20-22).

ABRAHAM He was called by God from his father's house.
He became the patriarch of Israel.
He became the Father of Faith.
He became the Friend of God.
He had an anointing of casting out barrenness.
He was blessed with financial and material prosperity.
BUT – the one thing he lacked was that he could not "cut out his lying habit," and it became a "generational curse" to his descendents – to the third and fourth generation (Genesis 20:1-7).

MOSES   He was called by God from the burning bush.
He performed ten national miracles in Egypt.
He opened the Red Sea with his staff.
He was a prophet and the deliverer of the Israelites.
He received the Ten Commandments from God.
He was so highly anointed; sometimes people could not even look at his face.
BUT – the one thing he lacked was he could not "control his anger" and it kept him from entering Canaan (Numbers 20:1-12).

SAMSON   Had a prophetic blessing from his mother's womb.
He had the anointing of might on his life.
He conquered the Philistines single-handedly.
He judged Israel for twenty (20) years.
BUT – the one thing he lacked was he failed to conquer his own "sexual weakness," and his lust for sex conquered him. He became blind and died a hopeless death (Judges 16:1-21).

ELI   He was the High Priest for the nation of Israel.
He had prophetic insight.
He had the anointing of knowing the voice of God.
BUT – the one thing he lacked was the "spirit of correction," or discipline toward his children. They all died and the glory departed from Israel (1 Samuel 4:12-22).

KING DAVID   He became King by divine elevation.
He killed Goliath and restored Israel back to glory.
He was a man after God's own heart.
He conquered the Philistines in all their battles.
He ruled Israel for forty (40) years.
BUT – the one thing he lacked was a "loving confrontation" with those around him. He died with a lot of skeletons in his closet (1 Kings 2:1-10).

SOLOMON   He had a vision of the Almighty God.
He was anointed with wisdom from above.
He built the first temple for Israel and the gate was called beautiful.
BUT – the one thing he lacked was controlling his "sexual lust for women," and it destroyed his kingdom (1 Kings 11:1-13).

ELIJAH   He was called the Man of God.
He prayed and it never rained for three years and six months in Israel.
He commanded fire to come down from heaven.
He eliminated 450 false prophets from Israel.
He was called the prophet of fire.
He was taken to heaven alive by an angelic chariot.
BUT – the one thing he lacked was "boldness against Jezebel," and it made him depressed (1 Kings 19:1-4).

GEHAZI   He served as Elisha's successor.
His eyes were open to see militant angels of fire on the mountain.
He gave proper information for General Naaman to receive a miracle from his leprosy.
He could have gotten a three-fold anointing.
BUT – the one thing he lacked was "discipline for humble beginnings." Instead, wealth brought a curse on him and his entire family (2 Kings 5:20-27).

JOHN THE BAPTIST He was a voice in the wilderness.
He officially introduced Jesus to the world.
He baptized Jesus in the Jordan River.
He saw heaven open and God's Spirit descending like a dove.
He boldly preached against King Herod's evil and corrupt moral behavior.

BUT – the one thing he lacked was guarding his heart against the "spirit of offence." He was easily offended and he died in prison (Matthew 11:1-6).

PETER   He was called by Jesus and became an Apostle.
He succeeded Christ in his earthly ministry.
He preached and three thousand souls were saved at one time.
His ordinary shadow healed the sick.
He structured the New Testament church.
BUT – the one thing he lacked was "overcoming prejudice and racism" in his own psyche. He was filled with prejudice and was bound by Jewish tradition (Acts 10:9-20; Galatians 2:11-18).

ANANIAS   He heard the audible voice of God.
He laid his hands on Paul and his blind eyes were opened.
He baptized the Apostle Paul into Christianity.
BUT – the one thing he lacked was "forgetting the past evil report" against Paul. He was bound with fear and lived in the past (Acts 9:10-19).

PAUL   He lived a righteous life even under the Law.
He got converted by Jesus Christ himself.
He became an Apostle to the gentile nations and witnessed fearlessly before Kings and Governors.
He wrote fourteen (14) books of the New Testament.
He wrought many miracles, even handkerchiefs or aprons from his body touched and healed the sick.
He established many churches in Asia Minor.
BUT – the one thing he lacked was "the spirit of tolerance." He could not be tolerant of others and would not give them another chance (Acts 15:36-40).

TIMOTHY   He was called into the ministry at an early age.
He was raised in a Godly prayerful family home.
He had Apostle Paul as his spiritual father.
He was ordained by Paul and other heroes of Faith.
He pastored the great church of Ephesus.
BUT – the one thing he lacked was "boldness" or "self-esteem." He was a coward, always afraid of what others would say (2 Timothy 1:5-7).

Life Application

Notice that all these great and anointed men were used by God. They had everything going for them, but there were some positive elements they lacked in their own lives.

Some of them fell by the wayside, others got shipwrecked in their faith, because of the "ONE THING THEY LACKED."

Identify in your own life that **pride**, **prejudice**, and **power** always cause men to fall, but humility will cause you to stand up again, or else it will be the "one thing you lack," and it will get you into trouble, or even destroy your destiny.

ONE THING YOU LACK

Chapter Ten

His One Mistake

He was born in a middle class home, where education, values, and hard work were taught and encouraged. And he did just exactly that.

After his college and university achievements, he climbed the corporate ladder and went to the top. He had financial and material prosperity in every area of his life. After that, he had fame and popularity above all of his peers.

He owned his own multi-million dollar company. He owned homes in various cities around the country and beside the beach. He ate the most nutritious and exquisite food and drinks. He took his vitamins every day and exercised at the gym four days a week. He saw his doctor twice a year. He never smoked or drank alcohol.

By virtue of all these good things in his life, he knew he would live close to one hundred years – until the inevitable thing of his life hit home – he died tragically.

His One Mistake Was
He Forgot God

- His one major mistake in this whole world was that he forgot God.

- He lived as if this world was all there is.

- He was successful in life, but he knew he was not satisfied within.

- There was a vacuum or emptiness within him.

The only one that could fill that vacuum or emptiness was Jesus Christ.

He had everything in life – but the "one thing he lacked" – was Jesus Christ.

> "For what will it profit a man if he gains the whole world, and loses his own soul? Or what will a man give in exchange for his soul?" (Mark 8:36-37).

The One Solution

The one solution regarding the emptiness of his soul was to have a genuine decision to accept Christ in his life.

Decision To Accept Christ

1) *Know That You Are A Sinner*

"You don't sin, and that is what makes you a sinner." NO!
"You are a sinner, which is why you sin."

Sin is in the genetic code or blood line of every human being on planet earth, including you.

"For all have sinned and fall short of the glory of God" (Romans 3:23).

2) *You Cannot Save Yourself*

Unfortunately, you cannot save yourself. There is nothing you can do to eradicate or wash away your sins. Your good deeds, charity, love for people, and financial support cannot save you.

"But we are all like an unclean thing, And all our righteousnesses are like filthy rags; We all fade as a leaf, And our iniquities, like the wind, Have taken us away" (Isaiah 64:6).

3) *Christ Loves You*

Jesus Christ loves you, no matter what kind of sin you have committed. Christ died and shed his blood on your behalf.

If you accept him today, he will wash your sins with his effectual blood and save you right now.

"But God demonstrates His own love toward us, in that while we were still sinners, Christ died for us" (Romans 5:8).

4) *Open Your Heart And Receive Him*

A gift is not a gift until you receive it. Christ died as a sacrificial lamb for you. Open you heart and receive the gift of his love.

Your heart is the core of your being. If you will open the door of your heart, he will come inside, sweetly and gently.

"Behold, I stand at the door and knock. If anyone hears My voice and opens the door, I will come in to him and dine with him, and he with Me" (Revelation 3:20).

5) *Confess This Prayer Loudly*

"Lord Jesus, I thank you for dying in my place. I know that I am a sinner, and I repent of all my sins. I ask that you wash away my sins with your precious blood.

I officially invite you into my heart to become my Lord ad personal Savior. Confirm your love by giving me peace in my spirit, and write my name in the Book of Life.

I thank you for saving me today, in Jesus' name I pray. Amen."

Congratulations, you are Born Again!

Please call me for further information at:

Tel: (718) 597-4403 or
Tel: (718) 324-5845

Or email me at
stephenlavoe@aol.com

We shall get back to you as soon as possible.

GOD RICHLY BLESS YOU.

AMEN!

Stephen Lavoe

OTHER BOOKS BY THE AUTHOR

1. Brokenness – The Release of the Oil in You.
2. The Ark is Still The Same
3. You are an Eagle, not a Chicken
4. Confessions

Best Selling Tapes and Videos by the Author

Eagle Generations
Weapons of Prayer
Mirror for Mankind
Stewardship Success
Distractions
Open Heavens
Depression
Prophetic Encounter
Excuses
Healing
Deliverance Encounter
… and many more.

For Books and Tapes Contact us at:

www.eaglesinaction.org
email – stephenlavoe@aol.com
Tel: (718) 324-5845 / Tel: (718) 597-4403

Address:
Action Christian Center, Int'l
4395 Byron Avenue
Bronx, NY 10466
U.S.A.

ORDER FORM

Postal Address

Action Christian Center, Int'l
4395 Byron Avenue
Bronx, NY 10466
U.S.A.
718-324-5845

Please send **One Thing You Lack** by Stephen Lavoe to:

Name: _____

Address: _____

City: _____

Telephone (_____) _____

E-mail _____

Book Price: $10.00 in U.S. dollars

Shipping: $3.00 for the first book, and $0.75 for each additional book to cover shipping and handling within U.S., Canada, and Mexico. International orders, add $5.00 for the first book and $2.25 for each additional book.

Quantity Discount Available - Please call for information

718-324-5845